SEARCH AND DESTROY

MW00336009

Also by Ted Rall

Waking Up in America
All the Rules Have Changed
Real Americans Admit: The Worst Thing I've Ever Done!
My War with Brian
Revenge of the Latchkey Kids
2024

SEARCH AND DESTROY

CARTOONS BY TED RALL

**Andrews McMeel
Publishing**

Kansas City

Ted Rall's editorial column and social-commentary cartoons are distributed in the United States and overseas by Universal Press Syndicate. For information, please contact: Universal Press Syndicate, 4520 Main Street, Kansas City MO 64111.

Search and Destroy copyright © 2001 by Ted Rall. All rights reserved. Printed in the United States of America. No part of this book may be used or reproduced in any manner whatsoever without written permission except in the case of reprints in the context of reviews. For information, write Andrews McMeel Publishing, an Andrews McMeel Universal company, 4520 Main Street, Kansas City, Missouri 64111.

Various cartoons in this collection have appeared in or been commissioned for non-syndication publication: *Time* magazine, *Fortune* magazine, *Silicon Alley Reporter* and *The Village Voice*. These cartoons, as well as those distributed through Chronicle Features (before September 1, 1996) and Universal Press Syndicate (after September 1, 1996), are copyright © 2001 Ted Rall, All Rights Reserved.

Ted Rall Online: www.rall.com

Much thanks to: Jim Aley, Ruben Bolling, Alice Chang, Judy Chang, Susan Chira, Bärd Edlund, Dave Eggers, Henry Goldblatt, Matt Groening, Ted Keller, Jon Landman, Randall Lane, Paul Levenson, Stan Mack, John McMeel, Toni Mendez, Terry Nantier, Tim Norris, Joel Pett, Julie Roberts, Lynn Wine, Sue Roush, Lee Salem, Bill Smith, Kenneth Smith, Larry Smith, Cole Smithey, Frank Tagiarello, John Vivona, Signe Wilkinson and, as usual, my mom.

01 02 03 04 05 BAH 10 9 8 7 6 5 4 3 2 1

ISBN: 0-7407-1396-5

Library of Congress Catalog Card Number: 00-108460

── **ATTENTION: SCHOOLS AND BUSINESSES** ──

Andrews McMeel books are available at quantity discounts with bulk purchase for educational, business, or sales promotional use. For information, please write to: Special Sales Department, Andrews McMeel Publishing, 4520 Main Street, Kansas City, Missouri 64111.

Foreword

As a kid, I used to read the newspaper end to end and follow everything I could about news and politics. JFK, RFK, and MLK were all blown away before I really started paying attention, but once I began, the hits kept coming: Vietnam, Nixon's resignation (which, with its frequent interruption of network programming, practically ruined my fourth grade summer vacation). Then came the '70s recession and the "oil shortage." In high school, Ronald Reagan got elected. I didn't mind so much his senility or innate cluelessness, but it upset me to watch him get billed as Mr. Conservative when, in fact, he was tripling the national debt. I really didn't get it. Around this time, I started noticing supposedly liberal magazines running leafy green ads by petrochemical-type companies bragging about the many favors they do for Mother Nature. And as the supposed battle lines and rhetoric about who stood for what were becoming increasingly blurred, it was also becoming clear to me that third parties never win, socialists drink too much and then kill themselves, and communists have a preternatural disposition to make ugly apartment complexes. The conclusion was inevitable: Politics are depressing, and everything is a big lie.

I'd always been inspired by Thoreau's "Civil Disobedience," in which he wrote that you should never participate in a system you think is wrong, that you should "Cast your vote not with a mere strip of paper, but with the whole of your being." Since politics seemed to be dominated by dirtbags, however, and since I could never decide for myself whether outright violence is a reasonable way to engage in the world, I decided not to engage whatsoever. Or rather, I adopted (unwittingly along with many, many others) a sort of autodidactic "silence, cunning, and exile" approach to that impulse-formerly-known-as-political. This meant that one should help old ladies cross the street, travel a lot, attempt to understand other cultures and types of people, treat all people equally, don't pollute, don't kill things, always recycle, and never buy anything new for fear of perpetuating a corrupt system. But above all, never talk about what you believe in, because doing so will lead to conversations with good but weak and self-deceiving people who try with ever-greater exertion to believe that mere intentions effect actual change in the world. To be seduced into these discussions by the need for community was ultimately to become bored and excruciatingly anxious about wasting time that could be spent doing something more helpful in the world.

This exile from politics left me feeling quite lonely. After all, it's kind of a dispirited way to drag one's ass through the world. So one night, laying around on the Bowery with a needle dangling out of my arm (just kidding. . . does anyone read forewords anymore?), I came across an article Ted Rall had written called "College Is for Suckers." The piece was about the financial and emotional realpolitik of borrowing and paying for college. The point was that "higher learning" is being steadily undermined by market and political forces to such a degree that for middle- to working-class people, blithely embarking upon a liberal arts education for its own sake is tantamount to semi-eternal perdition. In other words, Ted wrote, for the enlightenment you may or may not expect to get from immersion into Comparative Modifiers, Merkin Studies, Toltec Urban Planning, or Ashanti Womens' Perspectives, you'd better brace yourself for a decade or more of crippling debt, a job you hate, and a subsequent impairment of your ability to have anything resembling an adult life.

"Whoa, man!!" I said. Or something equally heavy. Because it was the first time I'd ever felt addressed in this type of discourse — political, socioeconomic, etc. — the first time I'd ever seen charts and statistics and analysis that explained my own life back to me. Ted's article was immaculately well researched, and it explained with all the authority of the so-called authorities I'd come to hate A) why my post-graduate school life sort of economically sucked and B) why the lives of many of my friends sucked in likewise fashion. And it did so in a funny, informative, helpful way. And so I became interested in Ted. Because Ted, by understanding our situation, made things suck less. Subsequent Ted articles proved equally educational and enjoyable. Not only were they fun, but they addressed a longstanding but hitherto unacknowledged need to feel that someone else out there was paying attention to the ways and wherefores of the various contributing suckages in my life.

I discovered that not only was Ted a writer, he was a cartoonist, syndicated in more than one hundred newspapers. Partly just as an excuse to get to know him, I called him up and asked him to participate in a book I was coediting called *Gig*, (a collection of interviews with people talking about their jobs based on Studs Terkel's *Working*). We didn't have anyone who was a cartoonist, and we didn't have anyone who was political, and Ted seemed like an interesting interview.

So that's when I got to see for the first time some of Ted's work, i.e. cartoons with titles like:
"So You're Dead. Now What?" "Kids Killing Kids . . . Kids Eating Children. . . It's Time To MAKE CHILDHOOD ILLEGAL!" "They Gave the Best Weeks Of Their Lives . . . Now It's Time to Honor VETERANS OF FOOLISH WARS." "Happy Shiny People You Know." "Yo, White Liberals! Get Guilt-Free Street Cred with Chet's African American Rent-a-Friend!"

I guess stuff either works for you or it doesn't. Ted's cartoons work for me. Partly because he's funny, and partly because he has come up with a way of skirting the largely irrelevant (or at least too tormentedly inter-co-opted) rhetoric of right vs. left, Republican vs. Democrat. This is to say Ted's cartoons rail not about donkeys and elephants, but rather they're about issues that have a recognizable influence and impact upon my life and the people I know: advertising, the dumbing down of the culture, the privatization of nearly every aspect of life, the growing disparity between rich and poor, the follies of late-stage capitalism, feminism, pseudofeminism, the bummer of being a "'tweener," the effects of divorce culture, friendships, relationships, the dissolution of various and once-recognizable social compacts under the weight of market forces, prescription drug culture, political correctness. I suppose this sounds like a drag — except Ted makes it really funny.

Only in a Ted Rall cartoon will you find "Julie McCane, the gay African-American Jewish woman who's making a real difference!" (and serves as nothing more than a lackey for the right).

Or the one with two guys, one presumably a boss and the other a troubled-looking employee, surveying a devastated environmental, post-apocalyptic landscape as the boss says, proudly, "Yeah, but think of all jobs that were created!"

Some of Ted's cartoons are topical. The recent Absurdicon in Kansas over teaching creationism in public schools gets a nice pimp-slapping in "Kansas School Board, 2009" which features Linus Van Pelt stridently voicing his right to insist upon the teachings of "pumpkinology." Others are just weird, existential, but somehow satisfying bits like "The Hypothetical Crisis Response Team!" and "My '60s Memories," which have no overt target so much as they express funny feelings you've had about various dorky, cheesy phenomena.

In Ted's comics, even the choice of a font can be funny, or the underlining of a single word for emphasis, the side details, the exaggeratedly gleeful shoulder posture of a shmuck gloating "YESSS," ignorantly celebrating the fact that his boss has just given him a pile of worthless stock options.

These are the kinds of things that make me laugh when I read Ted's cartoons.

Ted was the first person to teach me to passionately, histrionically, sportively loathe Baby Boomers for the black holes of American life that they often are, forever hogging first dibs on drugs, music, sex, and political power, dragging the entire weight of our economy everywhere they go, leaving the rest of us to fight among the shitty leftovers while disdaining us for being whiney. Ted's unabashed hatred for his loser father in *Revenge of the Latchkey Kids* was the first time I'd ever seen someone express publicly the anger that many of my friends feel toward their spoiled dads, who married, haphazardly begat progeny, then abandoned them in the tizzy of the self-centered '70s.

I still think it's a shame when people confuse talking about issues and politics with actually helping people. Talking like a liberal or an activist isn't the same as not polluting or putting an inner-city kid through college with your own money. But I guess I've learned (from my lonely, ineffective years on the Bowery) that there is a place for discussion. Especially if it's funny. It's sort of like antidepressants and therapy: Together, political awareness and actual, effective action can help you much more than either can alone.

I don't always agree with Ted's politics. But what Ted has done for me is make it easier to think and speak in political terms, to know that there are other people out there who think everything is as dumb as I do, and that there is some kind of eventual hope for forging discourse with action.

Because, as my interest in politics has slowly rekindled, I've realized that what happens when I, you, everyone we know, etc., say "fuck you" to politics, all that happens is politics says "fuck you" back. Which means that if you think people should be able to afford college, drink water without getting cancer, and work less than sixty hours a week to afford decent housing, or you simply don't feel great about standing by as a passive witness to racism, environmental destruction, et al, then, unfortunately, you need to set about the ugly, frustrating task of finding other people who feel the same way you do. It's a long haul, especially if you're out of practice. But if you can laugh along the way, it's a lot, lot easier.

—John Bowe

John Bowe, a freelance writer and filmmaker in New York, is coeditor of Gig: Americans Talk About Their Jobs at the Start of the New Millennium.

Introduction

I don't like to tell the story about my Big Break in Cartooning, because it's both a painful memory and it involves me acting like a big wuss. But here goes anyway; even such a low art as cartooning necessitates self-revelation, suffering and suffering through self-revelation.

It was February of 1991, when I was a twenty-eight-year-old college senior in New York. I went to a pay phone at the corner of 110th and Amsterdam to check my messages, and one of them was from an editor at a small newspaper syndicate that ultimately closed its doors five years later. I called her back, expecting less than nothing. I'd already been rejected by her and every other outfit in American journalism over and over and over. I assumed that she wanted to reject me over the phone (you'd be amazed how many editors like to do that), or to give me useless advice about my work ("Can you make it, um, funnier?") or to ask me the weather in New York as she packed for an East Coast sojourn. "I have good news for you," she told me. "We want to try to syndicate you." I dropped the phone and felt my knees start to give. Big tears welled up in my eyes. I'd spent five years working toward that moment, but somehow I mourned my loss—I'd invested an awful lot in being a failure, and I wasn't sure I wanted to give it up just yet.

It's hard to remember now, but 1992 was a very different time in America. We were entering our fifth year of a recession so hard and so deep that many pundits called it a New Depression, and George Bush looked poised to ride post-Gulf War popularity ratings to a landslide reelection. The Internet was something used exclusively by government employees and academic types, and something called the Information Superhighway was on a distant horizon. Grunge was the music du jour, and Gen X still referred to people born in the '60s and early '70s. If you want to know what it felt like to be young in America in the early '90s, think England. Life sucked, there was no hope of improvement and having a close circle of friends who all felt the same way made it all feel OK.

Nearly a decade later, I'm preparing to sign my third syndication contract. The same cartoons that got rejected by anyone with access to a printing press have found a mainstream audience in big-name publications. While not what it was a few years ago, the economy is still pretty damned healthy, at least if you're not poor, black, or live in a big city, and kids are dropping out of high school to take $70,000-a-year gigs crunching code for multinationals funded by twentysomething venture capitalists. We've got nothing but our great jobs and our bright prospects, and no time to hang out with our old pals. Most people are doing OK, but the increasing difference between normal mid-range American incomes and spectacular corporate executive salaries has gone from absurd to truly frightening.

But the weirdest aspect of our New Economy is the fact that the more we can afford to do something about the big problems (our filthy environment, systemic poverty, and our screwed-up health care system come to mind) the less we seem inclined to pay attention. It's the drowsy Eisenhower years all over again, complete with somnolent leaders, empty foreign threats, and escapist fantasies at the movies. People sometimes tell me that they envy my job. "Not only can you complain about things that bother you," they typically remark," but you can actually *do* something about them."

Of course, cartoons don't do anything of the sort. Contrary to oft-quoted cartooniana, Richard Nixon didn't fly back to San Clemente because he couldn't stand one more assault by Herblock. And while Boss Tweed may have found "those damned pictures" mildly irritating, Tammany Hall didn't collapse under the weight of Thomas Nast's scribbles for *Harper's*. At their very best, political and social-commentary cartoons (that's what I think of myself as doing) subtly shift one person's thinking on a single topic a little bit, one cartoon at a time. I don't expect to change a pro-NAFTA reader into an anti-WTO protester with my work, but if even one person begins to question their previously held convictions even a tiny bit, then I've been successful.

But I've also got another objective: I want to let people know that they're not insane. When I was a kid, punk songs by the Dead Kennedys, Clash, and Avengers told me that others shared my pessimism and alienation. Trust me; this is important stuff when you're a teenager in suburban Ohio. Similarly, my cartoons are a message to other people that they're not alone when they doubt that the president truly cares about them, that what's good for corporations is good for everybody, that we'll fix this global warming thing as soon as we figure out whether or not it's really happening and that true love really exists. They may not personally know anybody else who questions the way things are and wishes they could be different, but there's a tiny comfort in knowing that they're not alone. Insane perhaps, but certainly not alone. *Search and Destroy* collects my favorite cartoons from my second five years of syndication, as well as some oddities and miscellaneous work that I did on a freelance basis. They represent, in my opinion, the best cartoons I've done so far. They also capture me during a period of remarkable freedom; no political cartoonist in America had to worry about censorship less than I did. I hope that you'll enjoy the cartoons in this book at least half as much as I did drawing them.

Ted Rall
New York City, 2001

Our era is defined by mindless consumerism.

The '80s were over by the time my cartooning began, but the legacy of greed continues.

A classic example of cartoon cubism, in which I tried to make two points at once and ended up making none at all. Readers of the *Los Angeles Times* fixated on the "Taco Bell madness" line in the third panel while ignoring the piece's deeper implication: that whoever is powerful ends up oppressing whoever's weak.

Like many people, I like daytime TV talk shows. Like others, I'm obsessed with World War II. This got me thinking about how our culture would trivialize a guy like Hitler were he still alive today.

A paean to my wife, whose stubborn resistance to all things new made her a perfect candidate for this tale about a woman who refused to cross the "bridge to the 21st century."

This rumination about the human condition—especially the human refusal to change one's own condition—followed yet another in an endless series of conversations with friends stuck in dead-end jobs.

One of my favorite cartoons ever, this is a simplified retelling of the fate that nearly befell one junior-high school classmate and did do in an old roommate. Whoever said America doesn't have class?

During the Clinton years, there always seemed to be another reason to do nothing.

BEYOND COMPASSIONATE CONSERVATISM

George W. Bush ran and sort of won on a platform of "Compassionate Conservatism";
if there's ever been a funnier oxymoron, I have yet to hear it.

Black Americans subscribe to a lot of conspiracy theories, and white media types find them terribly amusing. But after four hundred years of systemic racism—still ongoing, natch—it would be unreasonable *not* to buy into the idea that whites are always up to no good.

On Jan. 8, Arkansas prison officials left Kirt Wainwright, 30, strapped down and hooked up to poison-filled needles while Clarence Thomas decided whether or not to stay his execution.

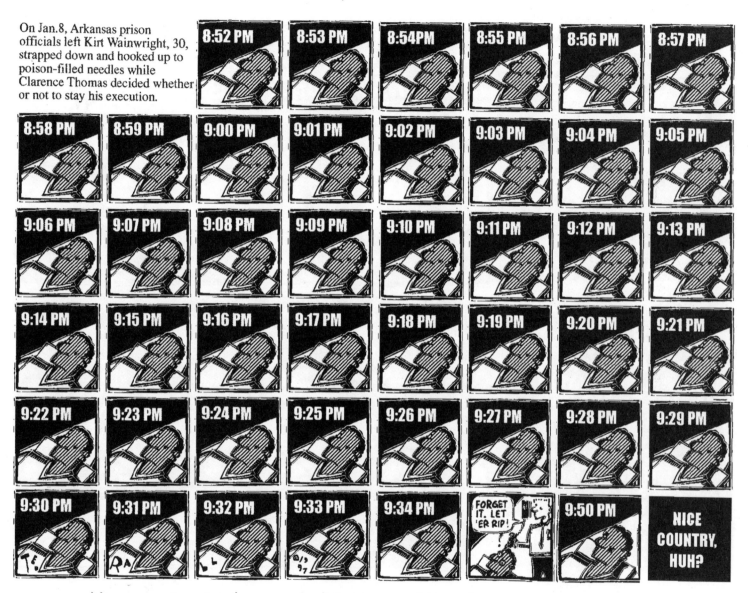

No one can imagine the terror that Kirt Wainwright must have experienced that night.

I KNEW AN OLD MAN WHO PUT UP A PLANT

THE PLANT HIRED PEOPLE TO MAKE STUFF

PEOPLE BOUGHT THE STUFF MADE BY THE PEOPLE HIRED BY THE OLD MAN WHO PUT UP THE PLANT

THE STUFF THE PEOPLE MADE AND OTHER PEOPLE BOUGHT FROM THE OLD MAN WHO PUT UP THE PLANT WAS MADE WITH STUFF THAT WENT INTO THE WATER

THE STUFF IN THE WATER KILLED THE PEOPLE WHO BOUGHT THE STUFF FROM THE OLD MAN WHO PUT UP THE PLANT THAT HIRED THE PEOPLE WHO DIED FROM THE STUFF THAT GOT IN THE WATER FROM THE STUFF THE PEOPLE WHO BOUGHT THE STUFF AND USED THE STUFF AND GOT TIRED OF THE STUFF AND THREW THE STUFF AWAY AND LATER DIED OF THE STUFF THEY BOUGHT

BUT I STILL DON'T KNOW WHY THAT OLD MAN PUT UP THAT PLANT.

©1998 TED RALL

An environmental variant on a classic nursery rhyme, as well as questioning the profit motive.

Fifty percent of Americans under forty have divorced parents, and most of them have been subjected to this transparently selfish argument at one time or another.

I've often wondered whether education budget cuts are intentional inflictions of ignorance rather than short-sighted neglect.

Inexplicably, thousands of otherwise attractive, sane Americans have begun wearing overalls in public. When will the madness stop?

After two years in the San Francisco Bay area, the smugness of the natives drove me back to the warm bosoms of those relatively less snotty New Yorkers.

Sometimes I wonder at the fact that couples can trust each other enough to sleep with each other.

Everyone wonders what might have been, but regrets are a major part of my life.

No, this isn't about me.

As incredibly screwed up as Gen X romance was in the '80s, today's twentysomethings have more fun at work than they do in bed.

This was inspired by the bow tie-wearing trust-fund editor of an ersatz hipster weekly paper who epitomizes a certain unsavory breed of dumbass who just won't shut up.

Just when you thought it was safe to go to the movies, someone makes another Laura Ashley movie.
Next up: George Eliot!

White people with dreadlocks: Why?

Perhaps the most offensive cartoon of mine to ever see publication in the mainstream press.
Failure to apologize is a recurring theme in my work—blame my dad.

MEET
★ JULIE ★
McCANE

THE CANDID CANDIDATE™

She's the gay African-American Jewish woman who's making a real difference.

PAID FOR BY PROGRESSIVES FOR McCANE

Legislative Record

- SPONSORED HR 313 "The White Power Reform Act" that legalized racism

- KEY SUPPORTER HB 242 "Family Values Initiative" that bans gay marriage

- VOTED FOR SB 4 "Holocaust Revision Act" that moves us into the future by deleting references to Nazism from school textbooks

Experience

- Has lived in the community since 1999

- Attended St. Regis boarding school, Yale, Oxford

- Led impeachment proceedings against perverted lesbian federal judges

COLUMN D

Here's what people in the community are saying:

BOB"ROBERT" JONES Chairman, **Better Business Bureau:** "I couldn't have built the new landfill without Julie. She gave us cover with the ghetto types."

JEFF M. BEAN CEO, Toxicorp: "Julie always returns my calls and she kept the environmental wackos off my ass. Mutations, schmutations!"

KEN "K." XAVIER, Young Rightist Brigade: "Just because she's gay and black and Jewish doesn't mean she's some sort of nut."

ON ELECTION DAY, REMEMBER JULIE McCANE

"I'll fight for the rights of the oppressed, the dispossessed and the depressed— just as I always have."

Just because someone's gender or skin color or sexual orientation is traditionally liberal doesn't mean that they are.

Disney pays its Haitian garment workers 30 cents an hour. This may not seem like much.

But, in Haiti, # LESS IS A HELL OF A LOT MORE!

Some people call us cheap for paying Third World workers low wages. But the cost of living in underdeveloped countries is incredibly cheap. $11 a week isn't much here, but by Haitian standards, it's an enormous salary!

But don't take our word for it—Check out what things cost in Haiti:

In the United States, this split-level 3-bedroom home might cost $250,000. But in Haiti, it's just *ten bucks!*

An average bag of groceries will put you out $30. But a Haitian housewife pays $30 to eat for a *lifetime!*

The new Mazda Miata starts at $19,200. But you can find it in Haiti for *$1.75!*

New Yorkers pay $60 a month for premium cable TV. In Haiti, they don't even have cable TV. *Cost: zero!*

Clinton and Dole will blow $600 million on this year's presidential campaign. But you could become the next ruler-for-life* of Haiti for a mere *$20,000!*

*Warning: May be revoked at any time.

THIRD-WORLD WAGES: THERE'S LESS THAN MEETS THE EYE.
A Public Service from your Friendly Neighborhood Multinational Corporation

TED RALL

Corporations justify paying low wages overseas by claiming that the cost of living is lower, but their paychecks are low even by local standards.

Formic existentialism meets the Beat Generation for no reason in particular.

"Mouse type" is the Madison Avenue term for those eensy-weensy warnings in commercials.

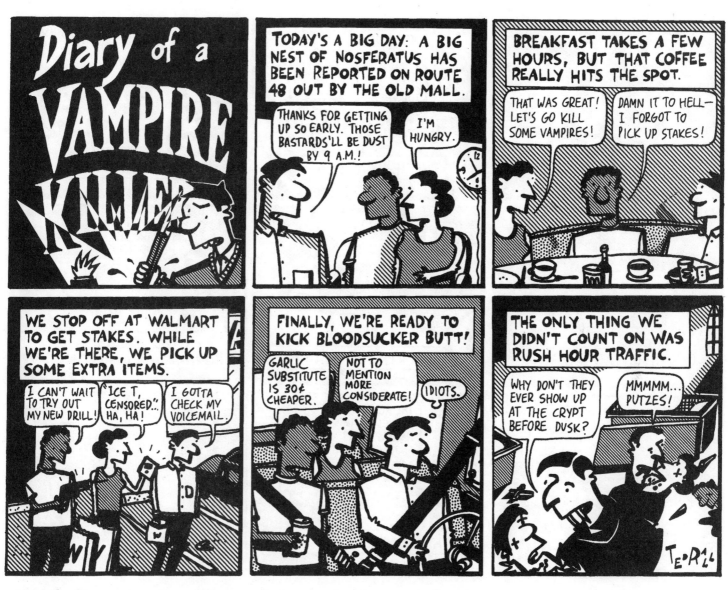

My wife, like me, is a fan of vampire flicks. But she always wonders why the vampire killers don't leave for the lair first thing in the morning.

What if your life was a made-for-TV biography?

I spent much of '99 pitching ideas to Hollywood executives. This cartoon is all I have to show for my efforts.

In the end, absentee dads skipped out on their families to have a good time.
Too bad it wasn't that fun for their kids.

Another warning label cartoon, this one in the aftermath of feeling betrayed by a fellow cartoonist.

My 60s MEMORIES

BY TED "MY NOSTALGIA REALLY MATTERS"

THIS MORNING THAT STUPID MRS. TAYLOR (WHAT A STUPID NAME HUH?) CALLED MOM AT HOME AND TOLD HER I FAILED MY I.Q. TEST. THAT REALLY WEIRDED HER (THAT'S MY MOM) 'CAUSE IN HER COLLEGE CLASS THEY TEACH HER ABOUT KIDS AND SHE THOUGHT I WAS SUPPOSED TO BE REALLY SMART AND STUFF.

$$\frac{2}{+2}$$

REALLY STUPID STUFF →

SO ANYWAY MY MOM SAYS, MRS. TAYLOR EXCUSE ME BUT IF MY SON IS BARELY FUNCTIONAL THEN WHY DOES HE HAVE STRAIGHT A'S IN CLASS? HOW DUMB DOES THAT MAKE YOUR OTHER KIDS ANYWAY? BUT, MRS. TAYLOR MUST HAVE THOUGHT ABOUT IT A LITTLE BECAUSE SHE TOLD MY MOM I WAS AN "OVERACHIEVER" WHICH IS SOMEONE WHO REALLY IS DUMB BUT WORKS SO HARD THAT HE COMES OFF AS SMARTER THAN HE REALLY IS.

ME → A- A A+ A- A+ A A. A+ A- A.

BUT THAT DOESN'T MAKE ANY SENSE BECAUSE HOW CAN YOU RUN FASTER THAN YOU CAN? OR CAN YOU LIFT MORE WEIGHT THAN YOU'RE ABLE TO LIFT? OF COURSE NOT! SO HOW COULD I ACT SMART BUT WORK SO HARD THAT NOBODY'D NOTICE THAT I'M ACTUALLY A MO-RON?! BUT MRS. TAYLOR IS EVEN DUMBER THAN I AM BECAUSE SHE DIDN'T GET IT AND SHE SAYS I NEED TO SEE THE SCHOOL SHRINK BECAUSE SHE'S WORRIED ABOUT ME.

THE SHRINK IS HERE

AT LEAST I CAN ALWAYS REHASH THESE EVENTS OVER AND OVER AGAIN, MAYBE IN SOME LAME CARTOON. I KNOW I CAN'T DRAW, BUT BY THEN EVERYONE WILL HAVE THE SAME EXACT MEMORIES SO THEY'LL GET A WARM FUZZY FEELING WHEN THEY READ THIS AND I'LL GET THE NEWSPAPER REPRINTS AND BOOK ROYALTIES AND ALL I HAVE TO DO IS END EACH ONE WITH SOMETHING LIKE A BROWN DOG BARKING GOING NUTS JUMPING UP AND DOWN AND I TAKE OFF RUNNING.

An oft-requested parody of Lynda Barry, the cartoonist who draws "Ernie Pook's Comeek."

44

45

This flashback to 1986 lovingly recalls an old roomie.

Actually, this is totally serious. Whoever first figured out that you could eat beets?
Of course, you can't *really* eat beets, but you know what I'm getting at.

The Internet: It just doesn't work.

Growing up in the Rust Belt means living with the detritus of past prosperity.

THE INCREDIBLE SHRINKING ECONOMY

The corporate-government complex always has a reason to say no to ordinary people.

At last, a solution to Guilty White Liberalism.

Thank God the military spent zillions of tax dollars to build the Internet!

The biggest problem Gen Xers face is that they don't think they exist as a generation.

You thought the Scopes monkey trial settled this one, but there are still schools in the U.S. that consider creationism to be valid science. Most recently, the state of Kansas ordered its schools to teach creationism along with the theory of evolution.

Every fall, husbands and boyfriends are dragged to an endless array of renaissance faires and medieval reenactments. Next up: the post-Renaissance!

Ever notice that the people who say "it's the thought that counts" never invest any thought?

If there's anything worse than being abandoned by a parent, it's having the asshole show up years after you stopped caring. Why are children of divorce nice to them? Got me.

There's a race of people—those who post online, pundits—who carefully analyze everyone's statements for ideological inconsistencies. Inconsistency is at the core of humanity, of course, but the inconsistency detection business is booming nonetheless.

Time magazine has given me an outlet for amazingly out-of-the-mainstream ideas; here's one of the ones they ran to my great surprise.

This Time cartoon never saw print, so here it is for the first time ever.

One of the few cartoons in which I express myself simply and succinctly.

Y2K mania went absurdly far; this cartoon appeared in *Time*'s millennium edition.

Our culture always concentrates on a tiny number of winners, but most of us are losers.

63

I'm a big fan of the *New York Times* obituary section, and this cartoon comes out of reading a few obits about, well, you know.

FORGET IRAQIS
IT ISN'T IRRADIATED VEGETABLES
STOP WORRYING ABOUT ILLEGAL IMMIGRANTS
KRILL IS HUMANITY'S WORST ENEMY!

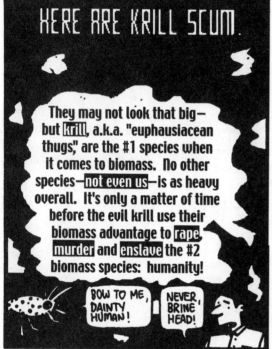

JOIN THE FIGHT AGAINST CRUSTACEAN HEGEMONY—EAT!

Paid for by Human Beings for Strategic Biomass Domination
A Subsidiary of the Fried Food Industry

"Native" meets "Starship Troopers" on the *L.A. Times* op-ed page.
This began as a rumination on obese Americans.

Sometimes a cartoon is merely about emphasizing a factor story that otherwise might disappear.
This cartoon is far better in its color version, but daily newspapers still won't run colorized editorial cartoons.

The Columbine shootings sparked a search for blame—while leaving the alienating brutality of high school culture off the hook. As with all things Columbine-related, I collected tons of hate mail from readers hilariously claiming to espouse pacifism.

More post-Columbine commentary.

Many cartoons by my peers and I have tackled this topic; nonetheless I still like the way this one flows four years after I drew it.

Pity the poor Oasis fan; liking the Brit-pop sensation is like surviving a UFO abduction.

This one is on newsroom walls all over America; editors loved this 1998 "Monicagate" cartoon but didn't dare run it.

The aging of the *60 Minutes* team is amazing to behold.

I often refer to Bush as George Quincy because he's as much of an historical afterthought as John Q. Adams.

RANDOM IMPULSES

ANTHONY SOMETIMES EXPERIENCED WILD, IMPULSIVE URGES.

THOUGH HIS IMPULSES WERE DISTURBING AND COMPELLING, HE WAS ALWAYS ABLE TO IGNORE THEM.

BUT ONE DAY WHILE HE WASN'T PAYING ATTENTION, A WEIRD URGE SNUCK UP ON HIM AND HE ACTED ACCORDINGLY.

THEY CALLED HIM A MONSTER AND A FREAK, AND THEY SAID HIS RANDOM DESIRES TO DO VIOLENCE WERE B.S. EXCUSES.

THEY SAID HE WAS AN ABERRATION, BUT HE KNEW THE TRUTH...

...SOMEDAY THEY'D GIVE IN TO THEIR OWN VIOLENT IMPULSES.

A classic example of what my first syndicate editor, Stuart Dodds, called my cubist approach; you can read this from either a pro- or anti-death penalty point of view.

74

Drawn after reading about an Arkansas inmate who requested that the dessert from his final meal be saved for the next day.

A scandal broke out during the winter of 1997–98 when it was alleged that graves at
Arlington National Cemetery had been sold to Democratic Party donors.

Boomers' complaints about the commodification of their youth didn't ring true
until K-tel started repackaging the '80s.

Killer asteroids! Alien invasions! Biochemical warfare! Why worry about real problems when there are so many theoretical ones to fret about?

It's not that I don't *want* to believe in God, it's just that the reasons people give for believing in God are so dumb.

It was hard for most voters to summon up any real passion for the Y2K election.

When you really think about it, a suicide pact requires a hell of a lot of mutual trust.

The entertainment industry is so risk-adverse that it prefers to recycle old ideas.

One of the strangest controversies of the late '90s was over the notion that "niggardly"— used by a white official in Washington, D.C.—was a racist word.

It's become all the rage to call people's voice mail to get credit for calling without the bother of actually speaking to them.

This *Dilbert* parody got me in hot water when the *New York Times* ran it on Father's Day.

IN TODAY'S CARTOON: AN EXCLUSIVE INTERVIEW WITH ONE OF THE CARTOONIST'S ACQUAINTANCES.

THANKS FOR AGREEING TO BE IN MY CARTOON.

HEY, THANKS FOR INVITING ME.

MY ACQUAINTANCE ISN'T JUST ANY 17-YEAR-OLD... HE'S THE FOUNDER, CFO, COO AND CEO OF MYACQUAINTANCE. COM, THE $3.4 BILLION WEBSITE!

ACTUALLY, THE BIGGEST PROBLEM I HAVE IS FINDING GOOD INVESTMENTS... HEH.

"I'VE ALWAYS WANTED TO DIRECT MOVIES, FLY A HELICOPTER AND MAKE A PLATINUM CD," MY ACQUAINTANCE SAYS. AND HE HAS!

LOOKS GREAT, BUT WE'LL HAVE TO AMEND THE CONSTITUTION FIRST.

FOR MPEROR

MY ACQUAINTANCE MET HIS "ANGEL", A 40-YEAR-OLD VENTURE CAPITALIST, THROUGH MY WIFE'S BEST FRIEND'S HUSBAND'S BUSINESS PARTNER.

NEEDLESS TO SAY, I'M A CHILD PORNOGRAPHER.

myacquaintance.com

NEXT THING YOU KNOW, MY ACQUAINTANCE WAS THE MOST FAMOUS PERSON NO ONE'S EVER HEARD OF.

DON'T GET ME WRONG: I LOVE MY GREEK ISLES, BUT IT GETS A TAD BRISK DURING THE WINTER.

IT'S MY ACQUAINTANCE'S WORLD, IF YOU CAN CALL IT LIVING IN IT.

MY ACQUAINTANCE... HE'S HERE THANKS TO THE MIRACLE OF NEPOTISM!

AND WHO DOESN'T LOVE THAT?!

The longer I've been part of the media elite, the more often I notice that puff pieces involve unsavory personal ties between the writers and their subjects.

There's a strange disconnect between a Fed that needs high unemployment to fight inflation and a WASP mentality that looks down on the unemployed.

Cop shootings of blacks in New York and Los Angeles hit the national consciousness.

More than 50 percent of eligible voters don't vote. The only question is, why do the rest of us bother?

AMERICAN POLITICAL IDEOLOGY MADE E.Z.

The economy boomed for quite a while, but the disparity of wealth has boomed even faster.

Incredibly, the flag-burning "issue" won't go away.

The only thing executives do is fire people, cut the wages of those who remain, and raise their own salaries.

OK, so equating Clinton with Hitler may have gone a little too far.

THESIS ENVY

After I wrote a piece critical of another cartoonist, his fans accused me of being "jealous."

Employers complain about labor shortages, yet still refuse to give raises.

The most dreary aspect of the Lewinsky scandal is the fact that all we got to *see* was guys in suits walking to and fro.

Our patented method proves it! Even a loser like you can

WIN A PULITZER PRIZE IN POLITICAL CARTOONING

You don't need to know how to draw. You don't need "ideas." Just take a famous photo and add labels to represent completely unrelated people, issues and abstract notions, and presto—you've created a Pulitzer Prize winner! Dozens of people have already earned as much as $5,000 using this simple method!

Yet another classic by next year's big Pulitzer Prize winner, Stewart Jacobs of the recently closed Baltimore Oxidonian. "The parallel between Jack Ruby and the Indonesians is as obvious as it is poignant," wrote critic Stewart Jacobs III (not Jacobs' grandson). Jacobs (the old one) gets a whopping $5,000 next year for an hour of work!

"We Hardly Knew Ye," Pulitzer Prize-winning editorial cartoon by Devon Schaffer of the now-defunct Chicago Daily Shepherd, 1971. This early phototoon won more than $1,000!

"Who's that guy with Robert Downey?" Rob Nilsom won the Pulitzer for the late NewYork Standard-Globe-Post in 1992.

This old photo from the Depression became something new and vibrant in Utah State News artist Dan Paulson's hands—and won him the Pulitzer Prize in 1994! Could you be next? Well, yes.

Want to know more? Send cash to: Kartoon Kash, PO Box 2092, Times Square Station, New York NY 10108

Political cartoons rely on increasingly absurd labels and forced analogies to make their tiny little points.

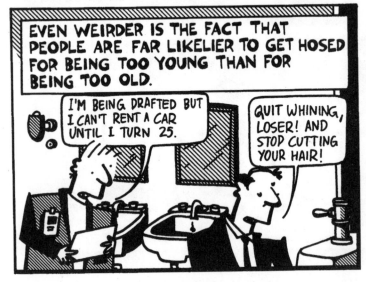

Age discrimination laws serve only to protect the old against the young; far more often it's young people who suffer from ageism.

ECONOMICS THROUGH THE AGES

The best part of surviving your parents' catastrophic divorce is that nothing much can phase you.

Despite mountains of evidence to the contrary, militant free-marketeers think that the lust for cash assures a perfect world.

FEAR OF A LATINO PLANET

NOW IT'S OFFICIAL — IN FIFTY YEARS WHITES WILL BECOME JUST ANOTHER MINORITY, AND HISPANICS WILL GO FROM 12% TO 24% OF THE U.S. POPULATION.

HEY **GRINGO**! I'M GOING DOWNTOWN TO DO YOUR WIFE!

WHAT THEN?

PROPOSITION 18,887 WILL STRIP CAUCASIANS OF THEIR CITIZENSHIP AND DEPORT THEM BACK TO THE UNITED KINGDOM — FORCING THEM TO GO UNDERGROUND.

HELL, YES I VOTED FOR 18,887! THOSE ANGLOS STOLE THIS LAND FROM US AND WE'RE TAKING IT BACK!

WHITES ARE A BAD INFLUENCE — LOOK AT THEIR HIGH DIVORCE RATE AND STUPID MOVIES!

ONCE-GRAND WHITE NEIGHBORHOODS WILL DECAY AS BUDGETS FOR THEIR SCHOOLS AND PUBLIC SERVICES ARE SLASHED.

WOT?! DIDN'T WATER USED TO COME OUT OF HERE?

I **HATE** MY WHITE-NESS!

WORST OF ALL, WHITE TV WILL BE RELEGATED TO COMMUNITY ACCESS CABLE!

NEXT ON CHANNEL 72 RHINO BOY

OUR ROLE MODELS BLOW!

PAYBACK REALLY HURTS.

SOON: WHEN PACIFIC ISLANDERS ATTACK

The weirdest side effect of unregulated capitalism is that it actually kills incentive.

It's like global warming; we'll deny the dangers of cell phones until it's too late to do anything to stop them.

White America always comes up with some lame excuse for racism.

Life is incredibly short, yet we're always told that change takes time.
For a race of mortals, dicking around just isn't acceptable.

Fortune ran my cartoons under the banner "Business as Usual";
I love attacking the stupidity of big business from within.

Somehow I wonder if my CEO readers understood the sarcasm here; several of them actually *believe* that they're being oppressed.

You'll know we've solved our problems with prejudice when people start being judged on their personalities.

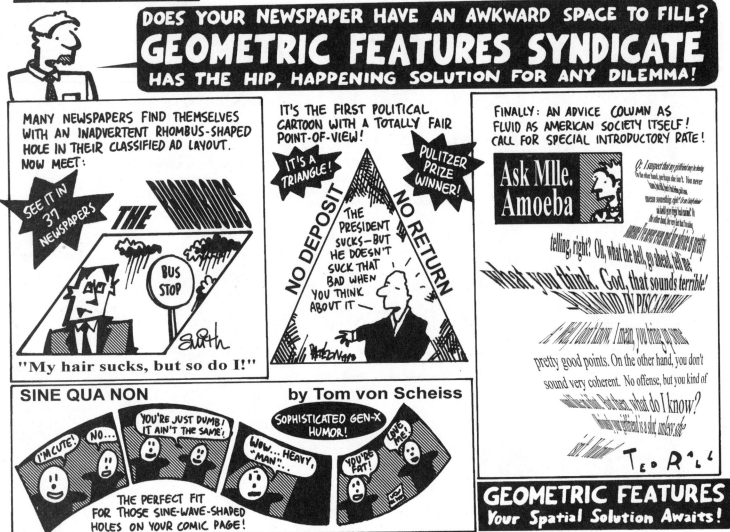

I did this one after an editor told me that he ran a rival cartoonist's strip for its convenient, easy-to-lay-out shape.

The 2000 census contained an unusual number of frighteningly intrusive questions.

IN THE TRADITION OF PINK FLOYD'S "DARK SIDE OF THE MOON," ITS WEIRD SYNCHRONICITY WITH "THE WIZARD OF OZ" AND VARIOUS CONSPIRACIES, HERE'S
MORE POP CULTURAL ODDITIES!

When I saw the story in the paper, I couldn't resist doing a cartoon about it. Angry pet owners complained that I was convincing their children that their missing pooch had been vivisected— never mind that this very well may be the case.

The end of the millennium called for a truly hysterical millennial cartoon; this one made crass history when both the *New York Times* and the *Washington Post* Web sites posted it. Now they read cartoons before they put them up.

This is the product of one too many chats with fat people claiming that their weight is caused by their "darned slow metabolism."

Life is a series of risks culminating in one last risk that ought not to have been taken.

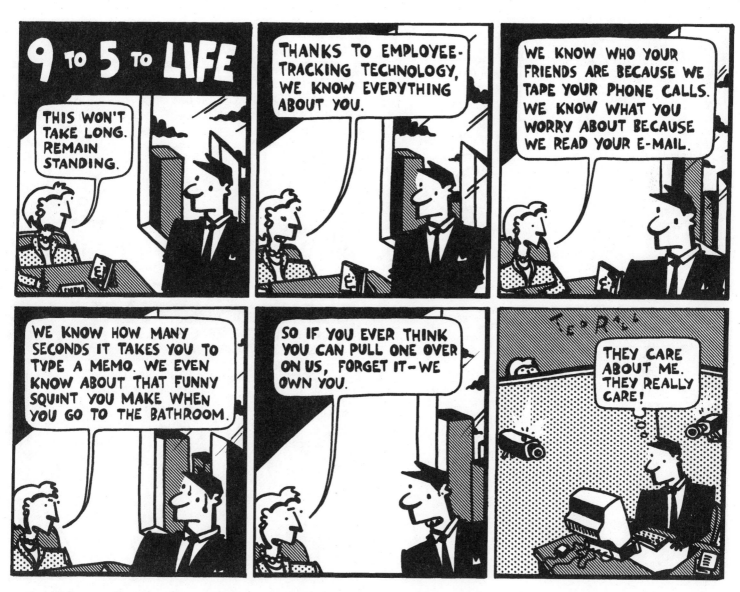

The balance of power has shifted so far from labor to management that workers mistake new-style control for old-school paternalism. Incredibly, most Americans don't object to sacrificing their own privacy to protect their boss's security.

Thanks to the miracle of genetic testing, American women are lobbing off their breasts on the off-chance that, maybe someday, they'll get cancer.

Kids sentenced as adults. Adults held years without trial. Executions where the victims burn to death slowly. Is this America or Afghanistan?

THEY GAVE THE BEST WEEKS OF THEIR LIVES... NOW IT'S TIME TO HONOR
VETERANS OF FOOLISH WARS

Tom Hanks is shilling for a World War II memorial, but what about guys who fought and died in the dumb conflicts no one ever cared about?

Kids are all on meds; we're all tanked. Maybe it's time to change a society when everyone in it needs to get wasted to get through the day.

DEFENSES FOR THE AGES : A PRIMER

Every year, droughts hit the south, wildfires rage in the west, and blizzards submerge the midwest. You'd think we'd be used to this by now.

I've done many of these "bosses like recessions because they weaken labor" cartoons, but this one works better than the others.

The awful truth: Nobody *really* cares about other people's problems.

TIME FOR A FOLLOW-UP: WHERE ARE THEY NOW?

One afternoon, while shopping at the enormous Strand bookstore in New York, I noticed a row of books from the 1910s by an author I'd never heard of. Obviously she'd been successful at the time, but now she was no one . . . thus this piece.

I don't know why, but the Internet seems to make ordinary people incredibly hostile.

THE GOAL OF BUSINESS IS TO MAKE PRODUCTS AS CHEAPLY AS POSSIBLE

THE BUSINESS THAT'S CHEAPEST EVENTUALLY CORNERS THE MARKET

THE THING IS, MAKING THINGS CHEAPLY MEANS SKIMPING ON DESIGN AND AESTHETICS, SO THINGS GET UGLIER AND UGLIER

PEOPLE SEE ALL THE UGLY STUFF AROUND THEM AND START TO FEEL UGLY THEMSELVES

UGLY PEOPLE THINK LESS OF THEMSELVES, LEADING TO THEIR ACCEPTING LOWER WAGES

WHOEVER SAID CAPITALISM WAS INEFFICIENT?

The "We're actually the same, you and I" cliché drives me nuts. But it's not quite as bad as the notorious reminiscence-of-lost-love-while-staring-at-a-music-box thing.

The real reason to notify neighbors when a convicted child molester moves into town is to save the cost of imprisonment—after all, criminals are either too dangerous to release or not. Anyway, few Americans could withstand such public exposure of their dark lives.

KIDS KILLING KIDS...
KIDS EATING CHILDREN...
IT'S TIME TO

MAKE CHILDHOOD ILLEGAL!

IT'S NOT BAD ENOUGH THAT "KIDS" GET FREE ROOM AND BOARD... PUBLIC SCHOOLS EDUCATE THE LITTLE BASTARDS ON YOUR TAB!

OUR FOLKS ARE AT WORK–WHILE WE WATCH TV AND DRINK THEIR BEER!

ADULTS ARE SUCH TOOLS!

THIS FIL IS RAT X

KIDS ADD ZIP TO THE G.D.P.—AND THEIR SLOTH IS COSTING US BIG-TIME IN THE GLOBAL ECONOMY.

I JUST WORKED A SEPTUPLE SHIFT, HONEY...WOULD YOU MIND MAYBE HELPING ME WITH THE LAUNDRY?

SORRY, MOM– I'VE GOTTA "PLAY"! HEE, HEE!

THEY'RE THE ULTIMATE SPECIAL–INTEREST GROUP: IMMUNE FROM EXECUTION AND EVEN PROSECUTION, CODDLED BY SYCOPHANTIC "PARENTS" AND ENTITLED TO "LOVE" FOR THEIR AGE ALONE.

I LOVE YOU.

I KILLED MOM AND NOW I'M GOING TO KILL YOU.

I LOVE YOU ANYWAY.

BUT AMERICA DOESN'T HAVE TO TOLERATE THESE DWARFLIKE PRIMA DONNAS. LET'S ELIMINATE THE PRIVILEGED ELITES AMONG US–LET'S MAKE CHILDHOOD ILLEGAL!

ONE, TWO, THREE, FOUR– ADULTS WON'T TAKE IT ANYMORE!!

ET RID OF KIDS

ADULT LIBERATION FRONT

NEXT: LET'S TAKE THE "YOUNG" OUT OF "YOUNG ADULT"!

MADISON AVENUE CATERS TO ME—AND YOU CAN'T DO ANYTHING ABOUT IT!

I COULD WORK...BUT I'D RATHER GET PIERCED!

The '50s and the '90s: The only difference is that our music is better.

Adults advise kids to take risks, but risks hardly ever pay off.

ELECTION DAY

I'VE CHECKED OUT ALL THE CANDIDATES' POSITIONS ON THE ISSUES. I'VE READ UP ON THE BALLOT MEASURES. I AM NOW AN INFORMED CITIZEN— AND NOW I'M GOING TO VOTE.

BUT NO MORE TRUDGING ACROSS THE STREET TO SPEND MINUTES OF MY PRECIOUS TIME IN LINE! TODAY I PLAN TO EXERCISE MY POLITICAL VOICE **ONLINE**— WHILE USING THE TIME I'LL SAVE TO INFORM MYSELF YET **FURTHER!**

CLIK

WHAT'S AN "ERROR -36"? BETTER REBOOT.

PING!

DAMN BUSY SIGNAL!

MR. T EXPERIE

BZZZT BZZT

HOW'S IT GOING?

THE URL'S FROZEN. I'M DUMPING THE CACHE.

MUCH MUCH MUCH LATER

I VOTED TO DECLARE WAR ON EVERYBODY.

THANK GOD NO ONE'S VOTE REALLY COUNTS.

TEOR 'll

In 1999, New York police shot Haitian immigrant Amadou Diallo to death under suspicious circumstances. This *Village Voice* cartoon wonders aloud about what might have been.

A cartoon retort to fellow cartoonist Tom Tomorrow, who denigrates voter apathy.

IN A MOVE CERTAIN TO DEVASTATE THE U.S. POLITICAL ESTABLISHMENT, WARREN HODGE HAS DROPPED OUT OF THE 2036 PRESIDENTIAL RACE.

AFTER CONSULTING WITH MY GIRLFRIEND AND MY GUIDANCE COUNSELOR, I HAVE DECIDED NOT TO SEEK THE PRESIDENCY.

HODGE (D-OH) MADE HIS DECISION AFTER HE WAS PASSED OVER FOR A NIGHT MANAGER POSITION AT A WAFFLE HOUSE NEAR THE I-75/I-675 JUNCTION.

GETTING TURNED DOWN FOR THIS PROMOTION MEANS THAT I WON'T SAVE ENOUGH MONEY TO ATTEND AN IVY LEAGUE COLLEGE WHERE MY ROOMMATES WOULD BE WEALTHY CONTRIBUTORS TO MY CAMPAIGN WHEN I'M 54 YEARS OLD. IT WOULDN'T BE FAIR TO THOSE FUTURE SUPPORTERS TO RUN AN UNWINNABLE RACE WHEN I'M DOOMED BY AGE 17.

PARTY LEADERS ENCOURAGED HODGE TO RECONSIDER, BUT HIS FOCUS GROUPS WERE CLEAR: HIS BID WAS HOPELESS.

YOU WERE OUR BEST CHANCE FOR '36—THIS MEANS 5 CONSECUTIVE REPUBLICAN TERMS!

QUIT WHINING! YOU'LL HAVE A DEMOCRATIC MAJORITY CONGRESS FROM '06 TO '28.

DOKKR LIVE IN FT. WAYN CD OUT NOU

WITH 2036 BEHIND US, WHAT'S AHEAD FOR 2040?

WELL, HODGE WOULD'VE WON RE-ELECTION, NO PROBLEM.

DON'T BE TOO SURE— WHAT ABOUT HIS PREDILECTION FOR IGNORING DOMESTIC POLICY?

NEW CHA

TED RALL

The outcomes of elections seem increasingly predetermined.
Would someone please explain what democracy and America have in common?

DIPLOMACY FAILED. BOMBING BOMBED. NOW LET'S

SETTLE IT ON DAYTIME TV

DRAGAN ALEKSINAC
Upset at forcibly being removed from home by Serb paramilitaries

SLOBODAN BYTYQI
Says his posse is "all that" and that Albanians are lame

In a postmodern culture where nothing is original and everything is derivative, analogy becomes everything.

Like the hitman in *Married to the Mob* says, I can't believe people do this every day.

As fans of my work know, miscommunication is a favorite theme.
I blame my parents' divorce; what's your excuse?

I was under the impression that therapy was supposed to explain your weirdness,
but most of us use shrinks to justify it.

Sure, there's plenty of legit blame to go around, but sometimes stuff just happens.

Teamwork is the ultimate corporate joke; if we're really all in it together, why don't all employees get the same exact options?

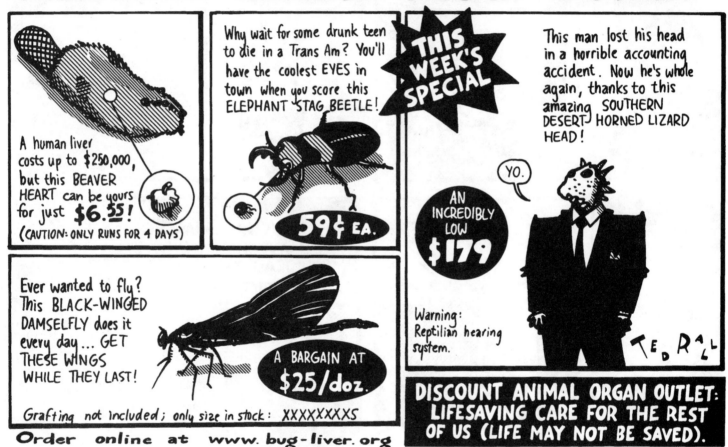

It's an appalling scandal: Americans die every day because they're not rich enough to buy a needed organ. So much for the magic of the free market.

IN A WORLD WHERE EVERYTHING ORIGINAL HAS BEEN DONE BEFORE, HERE'S THE LAST LEFTOVER SHTICKS

A postmodern critique of postmodernism: Does that make it popomo or just mo?

IN THE OLD DAYS, UNSIGHTLY GROWTHS WERE ZAPPED RIGHT OFF WITHOUT A SECOND THOUGHT...

WEIRD MUTATIONS AREN'T JUST BIOHAZARDOUS WASTE — THEY'RE BIG MONEY! JOIN THE SAVVY AMERICANS WHO ARE SELLING THEIR UNUSUAL DNA!

DON'T MISS OUT ON THE BIOTECH GRAVY TRAIN... CHANGE YOUR LIFESTYLE AND WAIT FOR THOSE LUCRATIVE LUMPS TO APPEAR!

This commentary about the '97 spate of disaster movies may be dated, but whatever.

We're hostage to the global economy—or so we're told. Most of us suspect, however, that it's just another excuse to underpay and overwork us.

I truly don't understand depression that doesn't follow some, er, depressing stimulus.

IF US AIRWAYS CHAIRMAN STEVE WOLF SUCCESSFULLY SELLS HIS COMPANY TO UNITED AIRLINES, HE'LL WALK AWAY WITH $123 MILLION FOR 4 YEARS OF WORK—MONEY HE GOT FROM CUTTING THE SALARIES OF 145,000 PEOPLE.

HOW CAN ONE MAN DESERVE SO MUCH?

FOR ONE THING, STEVE ALWAYS GETS OVERCHARGED FOR THINGS. REGULAR PEOPLE DON'T NEED AS MUCH JUST TO GET BY!

HERE'S YOUR CHEESEBURGER DELUXE. THAT'LL BE $14.2 MILLION.

WOT?! LAST WEEK IT WAS $12.1 MILLION!

ALSO, THAT PESKY STUDENT LOAN INTEREST CAN REALLY ADD UP!

REMEMBER THAT $2,500 YOU BORROWED FRESHMAN YEAR? NOW YOU OWE YOUR GOVERNMENT $2 BILLION. (WE ROUND UP FOR CONVENIENCE.)

BUT I NEVER GOT THE BILL!

AND WHEN HIS WIFE GOES SHOPPING? LOOK OUT!

I BOUGHT BOLIVIA.

THE FREE MARKET: TO EACH ACCORDING TO HIS NEED, OR GREED, AS THE CASE MAY BE.

Sure, it's an ad hominem attack, but it's individual actions like this that make life suck for everyone else.

159